LETTERS of the WEST

A Little Naturalist Book ©

LETTERS *of the* WEST

An **ABC BOOK** of the Many Plants, Animals, and Other Curious Features of the West

Written by Michelle E. Walch & John Maddin • Illustrated by John Maddin

First Edition September 2014.

Cover and interior design by Brian David Smith
Cover illustration by John Maddin

Library of Congress Cataloging-in-Publication Data

Walch, Michelle, author.
 Letters of the West : an ABC book of the many plants, animals, and other curious features of the West / written by Michelle Walch and John Maddin ; illustrated by John Maddin. -- First edition.
     pages cm. -- (Little naturalist series ; 2)
 Summary: "Flora and fauna of the wilderness is captured in this artistic alphabet book by author Michelle E. Walch and artist John Maddin. Filled with a variety of landscape marvels, Letters of the West invites younger readers to learn their ABCs through delightfully bold and whimsical illustrations."-- Provided by publisher.
 Audience: Age 4.
 Audience: K to grade 3.
 ISBN 978-1-940052-10-6
 1. Natural history--West (U.S.)--Juvenile literature. 2. English language--Alphabet--Juvenile literature. 3. Alphabet books. 4. West (U.S.)--Juvenile literature. I. Maddin, John, author, illustrator. II. Title.

QH104.5.W4W35 2014
508.78--dc23

2014008092

Printed in the United States of America

ISBN: 978-1940052106

Portland, OR
www.craigmorecreations.com

For Bahiyyih

A is for Alpenglow, when the mountains light up in a rosy hue before sunrise or sunset.

B is for Beaver (*Castor canadensis*), nature's building engineer.

C is for Cougar (*Puma concolor*),
the stealthy, stalking mountain lion.

D is for White-Tailed Deer (*Odocoileus virginianus*), browsing in the forest and hills.

E is for Bald Eagle (*Haliaeetus leucocephalus*), soaring high in the mountain air.

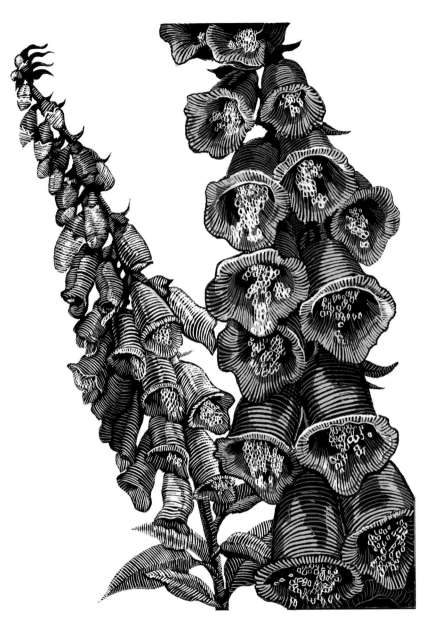

F is for Foxglove (*Digitalus purpurea*), whose flowers fit on your fingers and brighten your yard.

G is for Mountain Goat (*Oreamnos americanus*), whose feet hold firm to the mountain cliffs.

H is for Great Blue Heron (*Ardea herodias*), wading through the wetlands.

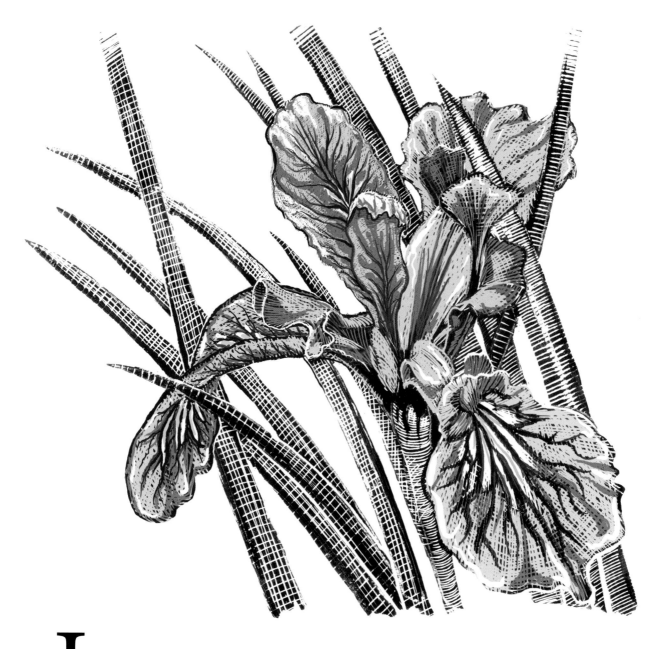

I is for Douglas Iris (*Iris douglasiana*), shining in the West Coast sun.

J is for Utah Juniper (*Juniperus osteosperma*), twisting as it grows on the arid hillside.

K is for Kinnikinnik (*Arctostaphylos uva-ursi*), also known as bearberry.

L is for Canada Lynx (*Lynx canadensis*), equipped with large feet for padding through the snow.

M is for Scribe Moth (*Habrosyne scripta*), fluttering in the night.

N is for Red-Breasted Nuthatch (*Sitta canadensis*), nesting in the mountain forest.

O is for Spotted Owl (*Strix occidentalis*), hooting in the old forest night.

P is for Prairie Dog (*Cynomys ludovicianus*), the black-tailed barking ground squirrel.

Q is for California Quail (*Callipepla californica*), California's state bird.

R is for Rose (*Rosa* spp.), resplendent after summer rain.

S is for Douglas Squirrel (*Tamiasciurus douglasii*), hoarding pine nuts and acorns.

T is for Trillium (*Trillium ovatum*), timeless three-petal beauty.

U is for Umbrella, ubiquitous in the rain.

V is for Turkey Vulture (*Cathartes aura meridionalis*), riding on the wind.

W is for Waterfall, cascading down from on high.

X is for Xeriscape, the low-water garden.

Y is for Yucca (*Yucca angustissima*), blooming in the desert spring.

Z is for Zigzag, Oregon, on the zigzagging road to Mt. Hood.